NEW YORK CITY
HAIKU

NEW YORK CITY
HAIKU

From the Readers of
The New York Times

Illustrations by James Gulliver Hancock

UNIVERSE

The editors of *The New York Times* would like to acknowledge the following *New York Times* staffers who worked on this project: Deborah Acosta, Jan Benzel, Bill Ferguson, Elisabeth Goodridge, Eba Hamid, Niko Koppel, Yonette Joseph, Matt McCann, Marie McDermott, Talya Minsberg, Jacky Myint, Andy Newman, Sharon O'Neal, Ken Paul, Alison Peterson, Emily Rueb, Dan Schneider, R. Smith, Daniel Victor, Amy Virshup, and Timothy Williams.

Published by Universe Publishing,
a division of Rizzoli International Publications, Inc.
300 Park Avenue South
New York, New York 10010
www.rizzoliusa.com

© 2017 The New York Times

Illustrations © 2017 James Gulliver Hancock
Cover haiku © 2017 by Robb Pearlman

Project Editor: Elizabeth Smith
Design: Lynne Yeamans

2017 2018 2019 2020 / 10 9 8 7 6 5 4 3 2 1

Printed in China

ISBN-13: 978-0-7893-3120-5

Library of Congress Control Number: 2016947896

INTRODUCTION

This book had its beginning in National Poetry Month in 2014. *The New York Times* invited its readers to write haiku about the city. In three lines of five, seven, and five syllables each, writers were asked to fashion their poems on the themes of "island," "strangers," "solitude," "commuting," "6 a.m.," and "kindness."

The poems we received in response to our challenge, more than 2,800 submissions in ten days, were as impressive as the city itself. A panel of judges drawn from the staff at *The Times* and New York State Poet Marie Howe chose their favorites, including those haiku in which some fundamental aspect of the city was recognized.

Each of the three-line poems included in this book moved us in some way, making us laugh, think, reflect, smile, blush, or even fume. Accompanying the words from *Times* readers are delightful glimpses of the city from the pen of the renowned illustrator James Gulliver Hancock. No stranger to the Big Apple, Mr. Hancock has been drawing every building in New York City since 2010.

By turns fresh, witty, and thoughtful, these haiku express universal truths about living and loving everything that New York City has to offer. We hope you enjoy *New York City Haiku* as much as we did, and share our delight in discovering how much our readers understand—and love—the city and its people.

—Amy Zerba and Dagny Salas

As we leave for work

Youngsters head home from parties.

Eras intersect.

AMPARO PIKARSKY, *Edison, New Jersey*

The New Yorker is

Not kind, they say. I say, he

Just left it at home

FLOR ARLEY HODGE, *Bronx, New York*

Crumpled states of sleep

First misty light on Hudson

The hamster wheel turns

PAMELA VARKONY, *Allentown, Pennsylvania*

There's not much twerking

Going on at six a.m.

On the ferry boat.

ROBERT D. DIAMANT, *Staten Island, New York*

Six-thirty a.m.

Pink sky and thickening buds

Birds chatter, it's spring

KIM PHILIPPS, *Bronxville, New York*

Hidden among the

Sleepwalking, caffeine zombies.

A morning person.

AIMEE ESTRADA, *Hyde Park, New York*

Too rushed to say hi,

Faces pass hurriedly by.

But Joy! The rare grin!

LINDSAY LIEBERMAN, *Manhattan, New York*

Just one train later

Would have made the difference.

He would have been there.

MARGARET GWYN DUNHAM, *Manhattan, New York*

I sketch on the train

Captive models dozing off

Please don't wake up yet

BARBARA S. MIGDAL, *Manhattan, New York*

Tourists in New York

Three abreast, strolling, chatting:

I want to shove you.

CAROLYN LENGEL, *Garrison, New York*

Sudden storm! He shouts:

"Hey—Um-brella, um-brella!

Now only ten bucks!"

MILLET ISRAELI, *Manhattan, New York*

Eight million people.

Looking at something ahead.

But no eye contact.

IRA LEVITON, *Manhattan, New York*

Too late for drinkers,

Too early for commuters,

Time for the runners.

MAS ICHIDA, *Manhattan, New York*

fish market morning,

a flourish of spring heat makes

the fine gill slits bloom.

AMY VO MAFFEI, *Washington Township, New Jersey*

All New York strangers

brought together by baseball

Yankees? Not me. Mets!

JAY GOLDBERG, *Manhattan, New York*

Drooling, snoring folk

Bobbing heads sway to and fro

Those subway sleepers

CAROL DAVIS, *Manhattan, New York*

Riding through the park

no daffodils blooming yet

—but unbuttoned coats.

SHARON ROUSSEAU, *Manhattan, New York*

Strangers become friends.

Shoe and paw prints show the way

around the dog park.

MARY E. MOORE, *Gladwyne, Pennsylvania*

Cabs dart in and out

I curse and push the pedals

on my wet black bike

GARY MOMENEE, *Durham, North Carolina*

There are places in

Central Park, where you see no

Buildings, only trees.

LAURA SEIGLE, *Manhattan, New York*

Crowded subway car;

no one knows me—a comfort

and an affliction

MAURA MONAGHAN, *Blauvelt, New York*

streets strangely quiet

glass towers cast rosy hues

parks host eager dogs

LAWRENCE T. CHOI-HAUSMAN, *Brooklyn, New York*

A moment of bliss

When tunnels steal our Wi-Fi

Quick glimpse of freedom

EMMA SOLOMON, *Hastings-on-Hudson, New York*

morning train, no smiles.

why? I imagine that each

person aches inside.

MILLET ISRAELI, *Manhattan, New York*

an island once far

now the center of the world

this New York City

MARK STEPHEN O'BRIEN, *Little Rock, Arkansas*

Rainy Monday, you

won't defeat my stilettos.

Red soles leap puddles.

MELISSA C. MORRIS, *Ayer, Massachusetts*

those who stand so close

on this eight a.m. train ride

remain so distant

BOB FINKELSTEIN, *Philadelphia, Pennsylvania*

Let us praise the one

Who squeezes through subway doors

Spilling not a drop

DAVID STOLLER, *New Hope, Pennsylvania*

Lurking underground!

Sweet sounds of a violin,

My ears smile at him.

SARAH SINGER, *Brooklyn, New York*

Crocuses are late

Only snowdrops have arrived

A slow train to spring

KIM PHILIPPS, *Bronxville, New York*

This concrete, these dreams

Crafted before I got here

Gone before I left

LIBBY MERRITT, *Manhattan, New York*

I walk near Times Square

Stop at crosswalk, look at map

Behind me, "Move it!"

RUSSELL HENDERSON, *Milledgeville, Georgia*

Major Deegan south

To Willis to FDR—

We're here with no tolls!

CHRIS O'CARROLL, *Emporia, Kansas*

If you buy the beers,

I'll buy kebabs. Let's call it

Insider trading

LIBBY MERRITT, *Manhattan, New York*

Dollar pizza joint

An oasis in New York's

Harsh desert of cost.

DENNIS FRANCIS, *Manhattan, New York*

curse the day I left

energy and awesomeness

now I Amtrak in

SUSAN M. CHAGRIN, *Fulton, Maryland*

If the F comes now,

I could get there, right on time.

But I'm still in bed.

JILL HELENE, *Manhattan, New York*

Subway circus act

Feats performed on silver poles

Jaded faces melt

ALEXANDRA FORBES, *Wingdale, New York*

Brought my old guitar

to scream with on St. Mark's Place—

Where are all the punks?

ALLAN ANDRE, *Queens, New York*

Union Square Market

Blueberries for ten dollars

New York City blues

SHARON COHEN, *Dallas, Texas*

Oh, the New Yorkers.

They are not really strangers,

they are just themselves.

GEORGIA STAPLETON, *Shawano, Wisconsin*

dawn lights up the day

models seeking cameras

fashion still alive

EDWARD MURCHIE, *Great Falls, Virginia*

Grand Central echoes

muffled voices and footsteps

Metro-North awaits

CAROL SLOCUM, *Greenwich, Connecticut*

Lady Liberty

Shines with green springtime treasure

Of honor and faith

JOYANNE O'DONNELL, *Emmitsburg, Maryland*

Pockets of free space

in the center of the car,

taunting us sardines.

SIMONE BLASER, *Brooklyn, New York*

Strangers that I know

Emptiness of a full train

Do they see my pain?

JOHN MCCARTHY, *New Rochelle, New York*

Ah choo: Bless you, Sir

Excuse me; Thank you; Sorry

Would you like a seat?

VERONICA THOMAS, *Queens, New York*

Auto, boat, bus, train.

It's New York island hopping!

Tan not included.

COLLEEN TREMONT, *Manhattan, New York*

My hand on your hand

Your face a whisper from mine

For one stop only

ISABEL MARTIN, *Brooklyn, New York*

Crowded train. We bump.

She squares off. I roll my eyes.

Head cock. Pause. Smile. Smile.

KIKI BOWMAN, *Brooklyn, New York*

Park at Winter dawn

We danced through each orange gate

Unconcealing Spring

JEFF TAYLOR, *Nelson, New Hampshire*

Flood watch in effect

Commuting in wintry mix

Don't slip on the stairs

ROBERT ANDERSEN, *Jersey City, New Jersey*

Who are these people

Who smilingly give money

To Times Square Elmos?

DORIAN DEVINS, *Manhattan, New York*

On the roof, standing,

flying his kite in the sky

the street disappears.

EUGENE DUNSCOMB, *Southbury, Connecticut*

Homeless gentleman

White cane seeks safe street crossing

Teenage boy takes arm

JUDITH P. SMITH, *Halifax, Nova Scotia, Canada*

I would take a G,

And ride in the smelly car,

to be close to you

JEFFREY YURCAN, *Philadelphia, Pennsylvania*

Dodgers beat the Yanks

October of '55.

"Glory Days," Springsteen!

ROBERT D. DIAMANT, *Staten Island, New York*

We are all of us

waiting, wanting, wondering,

local or express.

ADAM BARD, *Brooklyn, New York*

Chill tempest at dawn,

Cab soaks with a puddle, still,

Spring breeze like champagne.

DAN STACKHOUSE, *Manhattan, New York*

Packed subway morning

Field trip of loud kids step in

This is my nightmare

STEVE POLESCHUK, *Brooklyn, New York*

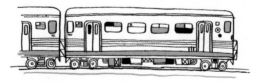

The City's timeless,

But still, don't let it fool you.

It's never the same.

LARRY GARLAND, *New Rochelle, New York*

It's easy for her

to sniff a stranger when I'm

left holding the bag.

DAVID SCHROEDER, *Manhattan, New York*

I give a free swipe

to a stranger since I have

unlimited time.

SONIA HALBACH, *Manhattan, New York*

I'm in a new world.

There's millions of strangers here.

Love, Me, from New York.

GEORGIA STAPLETON, *Shawano, Wisconsin*

Sweet scent of decay

slow wafts through a city's fumes;

6 a.m. pick-up.

SALLIE MCKENNA, *San Francisco, California*

Sparrows come and eat

the line of seeds left there by

the old man whistling

ELÉNA RIVERA, *Manhattan, New York*

crown heights two train to

manhattan to the bronx to

bus to work and back

KATRINA BROWN, *Brooklyn, New York*

59

Crick in my neck from

sipping this ice-cold coffee.

L Train, where are you?

KRISTINA MUELLER, *Brooklyn, New York*

Cherry blossoms wait

for Roosevelt Island to

break from winter's clutch

JAMES STARACE, *Manhattan, New York*

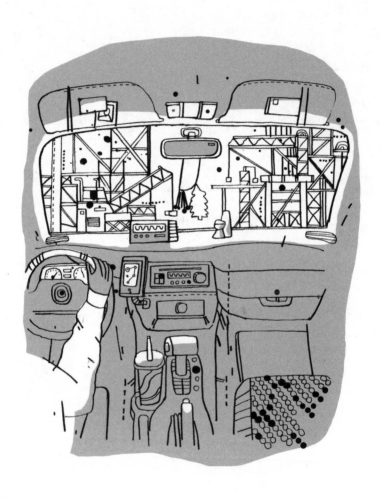

A sad, old cabbie

Telling about his divorce

I listen and nod

JESSICA PERL, *Kagoshima, Japan*

"Can you spare a dime?"

he politely said to her.

"No," she says, no shame.

MARGARET GWYN DUNHAM, *Manhattan, New York*

The day JFK

died, the subway was jammed, but

no one was speaking.

ALAN TEPLITSKY, *Lawrenceville, New Jersey*

Flakes of mottled skin

from upturned shoe fall, a light

dusting on pale blue

JANINE STANKUS, *Queens, New York*

Yes, it's an island!

Look at that lit-up palm tree

Right on 46th.

AMPARO PIKARSKY, *Edison, New Jersey*

I will talk to you

At parties, classes, and brunch

But not on the train

ALEXANDRA SVOKOS, *Manhattan, New York*

Walk in the City

Can't ignore the outstretched hands

Give kind words and food

ANANDA CAPOBIANCO, *Yonkers, New York*

across the platform

a slant of spring light slipping

through the subway grate

SUSAN RUDNICK, *Pleasantville, New York*

she hands me Kleenex

tears stream quicker down my cheeks

on the two / thank you

KATRINA BROWN, *Brooklyn, New York*

First shorts of the year

Spied on walk to Metro-North

On a brave student

KIM PHILIPPS, *Bronxville, New York*

We can spend the night

together, but I expect

bagels in morning.

NATASHA MCGLYNN, *Washington, D.C.*

I have a dollar

But I'm saving it for you,

L Train drum couple.

SARAH SHANFIELD, *Brooklyn, New York*

Bottles, sticky cans—

5 cents at a time you pick.

Here's mine and five bucks.

SIU LO, *Manhattan, New York*

I commute to school

then go back home with pressure

on my mind: future.

JOSE GUTIERREZ, *Bronx, New York*

Pizza with a fork?

DeBlasi OH MY GOODNESS!!!!!!

Go to Confession!

ROBERT D. DIAMANT, *Staten Island, New York*

The deli where you

and I ate hot pastrami

is a Chase bank now

LAURA BARANIK, *Queens, New York*

On the 6 to Spring

two cops help a tourist whose

map is upside down

FRANCES RICHEY, *Manhattan, New York*

I lost my headphones

but found that the subway had

music of its own

SCOTT PERCELAY, *Manhattan, New York*

Homeless man on train.

He sat there staring at me.

Do I look okay?

MARGARET GWYN DUNHAM, *Manhattan, New York*

cab driver Ahmed

used to be an engineer

American dream?

MILLET ISRAELI, *Manhattan, New York*

I see all of you

And you see me sitting here

We all stare ahead

MAX COHEN, *Brooklyn, New York*

Circular hole in

My MetroCard; bigger hole

where you used to be

MAURA MONAGHAN, *Blauvelt, New York*

Woman falls on street.

Crowd of ambitious strangers

Competes to help her.

ALISON KLINGLER, *Chicago, Illinois*

By the boat basin

Gunshots break the river's calm

Phew, film crew at work

BARBARA S. MIGDAL, *Manhattan, New York*

your curtain's open.

I see you reading in bed,

but don't know your name.

MILLET ISRAELI, *Manhattan, New York*

Matching blue flickers—

Watching TV together

on floors 10 and 4

ISABEL MARTIN, *Brooklyn, New York*

Elderly couple,

On Circle Line for a date,

Giving love a chance.

NURIT ISRAELI, *Manhattan, New York*

I just want some lunch.

Been riding this train all day!

Katz's! Here I come!

ALEXANDER FREDERICK SPILBERG,
Manhattan, New York

Face seen across tracks,

We stare, and a train passes,

Face gone forever.

HILLEL ROSENSHINE, *Manhattan, New York*

I hear them fighting

Through the thin wall between us—

but I don't take sides.

NURIT ISRAELI, *Manhattan, New York*

Our eyes avoid but

If we looked we would see that

We might just be friends.

SARAH LENAGHAN, *Brooklyn, New York*

Trees. Grass. Birds of prey.

Garden in bloom. Placid pond.

Lost in Central Park

MILLET ISRAELI, *Manhattan, New York*

If jackhammers wrote

Code, our Island would launch a

Facebook every day.

LAURA SEIGLE, *Manhattan, New York*

do not block the doors

do not lean against the doors

playing Candy Crush

TIM SACHS, *Brooklyn, New York*

The pizzeria

Shining near and oh so far

New York is a star

JOYANNE O'DONNELL, *Emmitsburg, Maryland*

89

The bag is moving

Everyone on the train looks

Out pops a puppy

JOAN MARTINEZ, *Manhattan, New York*

this city's a place

where a stranger's shoulder pad

may be a chin rest

PETER VALENTINE, *Brooklyn, New York*

Lonely in the night

Alone on a crowded train

Many hearts, one soul

JOHN MCCARTHY, *New Rochelle, New York*

The free subway breeze

is notorious to please

when spring is in bloom

JOYANNE O'DONNELL, *Emmitsburg, Maryland*

walk in late, cat mad.

"I'm sorry, Snoop, train trouble."

feels good to be missed.

MARGARET GWYN DUNHAM, *Manhattan, New York*

There she stands alone,

on her little island place.

Lady with a crown.

GEORGIA STAPLETON, *Shawano, Wisconsin*

Skyscraper starlight

Bids goodnight to tie-dye skies

In neon Times Square

KAREN MAQUILAN, *West New York, New Jersey*

Beware the puddle

of indeterminate depth

that swallows boots whole

MARY M. SUK, *Queens, New York*

Adrift in a sea.

We're all in this together.

We won't let you drown.

ALEXANDER FREDERICK SPILBERG,
Manhattan, New York

Drummers on the train

Pounding my headache away.

I gave them a buck.

MARGARET GWYN DUNHAM, *Manhattan, New York*

The snow piles are gone

And reveal abandoned trash

In the morning light

KIM PHILIPPS, *Bronxville, New York*

Beautiful woman

Laughs with me for a minute,

Subway takes her south.

DAN STACKHOUSE, *Manhattan, New York*

Rent: too high for me.

I'm forced to move to Jersey

where no one visits.

MEGAN HAUSER, *Brooklyn, New York*

table for just one

still searching for my lover

dessert must be fun

EDWARD MURCHIE, *Great Falls, Virginia*

Insomniac rock

Awake to the world, and smug:

Only one New York!

PAMELA HARDESTY, *Kinsale, Ireland*

Eye lock with stranger!

Will human beings connect?

Nope . . . they both move on.

PHYLLIS R. CHARNEY, *Manhattan, New York*

Subway tracks at night

Patter of leftover rain

Or rat feet, maybe

LAURA BARANIK, *Queens, New York*

Hey Mister Softee

Stop playing that jingle now

I won't buy from you

ELIZABETH MINEY, *Queens, New York*

"Still a neighborhood,"

He smiles—Yiddish memories,

Spanish in the air

CHRIS O'CARROLL, *Emporia, Kansas*

subway to the beach

two strangers in the first car

comparing surfboards.

JEFFREY RABKIN, *Manhattan, New York*

Kindness is when we

Lean on each other's shoulders

On the subway pole

SARAH LENAGHAN, *Brooklyn, New York*

Young, blind, they collide

His dog guides him around her

Oh, what could have been . . .

LIZ SIPPIN, *Fairfield, Connecticut*

On Skyscraper Isle

Where giants and homeless meet

But the world resolves

ETHAN GORDON, *New Orleans, Louisiana*

No Man's an Island

Not on the Morning F Train

Why Hello Armpit.

JASON PAUL, *Brooklyn, New York*

Strange how fast night comes:

Silence, as I pass through you,

wide awake at dark.

KAITLIN DUFFY, *Brooklyn, New York*

Behind him a trail

of bread crumbs, popcorn and seeds.

He makes birds happy

GERARD MIDDLETON, *Brooklyn, New York*

Deep in the darkness

Stranger's eyes meet feinted smiles

Rush through New York veins

MARIA V. MANON, *Manhattan, New York*

If Atlas held our

Island and anger turned to

Lead, he would drop it.

LAURA SEIGLE, *Manhattan, New York*

Country morning—here!

Birds chatter, church bells toll . . . then:

wailing car alarms.

PHYLLIS R. CHARNEY, *Manhattan, New York*

Alarms blare at dawn

Frantically rushing to dress

Wait, it's Saturday

ANGELA BONE, *Manhattan, New York*

six a.m. commute

a city of rectangles . . .

except for the clocks

ALAN S. BRIDGES, *Littleton, Massachusetts*

Sandwiched between men

I ride the packed subway car

"Is that your hand, creep?"

LIZ SIPPIN, *Fairfield, Connecticut*

Lone pigeon bobbles

Garbage cans rattle and clash

Dawn at Spring & Mott

CAROL SLOCUM, *Greenwich, Connecticut*

morning Q commute

has the best smell of the day:

coffee and shampoo

VANESSA VICHIT-VADAKAN, *Berkeley, California*

water surrounding

a universe in the world

tethered by bridges

RC DEWINTER, *Haddam, Connecticut*

If build and destroy

Are music notes, our island

Is a symphony.

LAURA SEIGLE, *Manhattan, New York*

"Insufficient fare!"

But, without saying a word,

stranger swipes me in.

JANET GOTTLIEB, *Brooklyn, New York*

The seal at the zoo

Applauds the passersby, arf!

I put down my book.

DENNIS SULLIVAN, *Voorheesville, New York*

It's the sweet shy glance

From a stranger on a train

That makes us happy.

DAVID SCHROEDER, *Manhattan, New York*

Red Hook Terminal:

cranes like life-size Legos loom;

the future does, too.

SIMONE BLASER, *Brooklyn, New York*

"Les Miz" one more time?

What? Sold out through the summer!

"Rocky" it will be.

ROBERT D. DIAMANT, *Staten Island, New York*

The neon orange

Of the kids' cheese dust fingers

All over this pole

SARAH SHANFIELD, *Brooklyn, New York*

Words dance on paper

Murmuring, screeching metal

A thousand arms sway

JESSICA VELEZ, *Queens, New York*

The man shouts his need

He has no home, food, or leg

His chair rumbles through

STEPHANIE WALTER, *Bay Shore, New York*

Coney Island gulls

Boardwalk, burlesque, hot hot dogs

Sunrise, thick red grease

ANNA DIVITO, *Westtown, New York*

Tall island lady,

welcoming all who come here.

Oh, New York! Freedom!

GEORGIA STAPLETON, *Shawano, Wisconsin*

are you, now, alone

waiting for the sun to rise

over Brooklyn Bridge?

AMANDA TUREN, *Manhattan, New York*

The apple grows big

pregnant with the promises

strangers never keep

MARTIN THOMAS, *Bergen op Zoom, Netherlands*

Coffee by myself

The wind whispers names of friends

Yet alone I sit

CAMILO DURR, *Manhattan, New York*

I know you, don't I?

You were me five years ago,

Dreaming of New York.

ADAM BARD, *Brooklyn, New York*

THE NEW YORK TIMES (www.NYTimes.com) is one of the world's most influential news organizations with fifty news bureaus around the New York region, the nation, and the globe. *The Times* is known for accuracy, depth, and authority and produces award-winning journalism, breaking news coverage, and opinion and commentary along with deep databases of content and rich multimedia presentations. *The Times* has won 119 Pulitzer Prizes and Citations, far more than any other news organization.

JAMES GULLIVER HANCOCK (www.jamesgulliverhancock.com) is an internationally noted illustrator, known for his playful drawings and as author of books including *All the Buildings in New York, 20 Ways to Draw a Bike*, and *Artists, Writers, Thinkers, Dreamers*.